The National Poetry Series was established in 1978 to ensure the publication of five collections of poetry annually through five participating publishers. The Series is funded annually by Amazon Literary Partnership, William Geoffrey Beattie, the Gettinger Family Foundation, Bruce Gibney, HarperCollins Publishers, The Stephen and Tabitha King Foundation, Padma Lakshmi, Lannan Foundation, Newman's Own Foundation, Anna and Olafur Olafsson, Penguin Random House, the Poetry Foundation, Amy Tan and Louis DeMattei, Amor Towles, Elise and Steven Trulaske, and the National Poetry Series Board of Directors.

THE NATIONAL POETRY SERIES WINNERS
OF THE 2021 OPEN COMPETITION

Symmetry of Fish by Su Cho
Chosen by Paige Lewis for Penguin Books

Harbinger by Shelley Puhak
Chosen by Nicole Sealey for Ecco

Extinction Theory by Kien Lam
Chosen by Kyle Dargan for University of Georgia Press

Ask the Brindled: Indigiqueer Poetry from Hawai'i by Noukahauoli Revilla
Chosen by Rick Barot for Milkweed Editions

Relinquenda by Alexandra Lytton Regalado
Chosen by Reginald Betts for Beacon Press

Extinction Theory

Extinction Theory

Kien Lam

The University of Georgia Press

ATHENS

Published by the University of Georgia Press
Athens, Georgia 30602
www.ugapress.org
© 2022 by Kien Lam
All rights reserved
Designed by Rebecca A. Norton
Set in 11/14 Palatino
Printed and bound by Sheridan Books, Inc.
The paper in this book meets the guidelines for
permanence and durability of the Committee on
Production Guidelines for Book Longevity of the
Council on Library Resources.

Most University of Georgia Press titles are
available from popular e-book vendors.

Printed in the United States of America
22 23 24 25 26 P 5 4 3 2 1

Library of Congress Cataloging-in-Publication Data
Names: Lam, Kien, author.
Title: Extinction theory : poems / Kien Lam.
Description: Athens : The University of Georgia Press, [2022] |
Series: The national poetry series
Identifiers: LCCN 2022021914 | ISBN 9780820362731
(paperback ; alk. paper) | ISBN 9780820362748 (ebook)
Subjects: LCGFT: Poetry.
Classification: LCC PS3612.A543284 E98 2022 |
DDC 811/.6—dc23/eng/20220506
LC record available at https://lccn.loc.gov/2022021914

Contents

III.

Extinction Theory

露の世は露の世ながらさりながら

The world of dew
Is the world of dew
And yet, and yet—

—*Kobayashi Issa*

Lunar Mansions

It matters where you are born. *In a barn*
means you are the holy star. Meteor child.

Jesus was the first bomb. *Where are you from*
is a question I field too much. Once

I said *Vietnam* and the white man said *I fought*
there. I loved the country. I love their people.

That was the day I started to lie
about my birth. *In the stable*

the horses kicked me from their wombs.
It was exactly like finding a baby

in a haystack. It was snowing
in Michigan when the priest exorcised me

from my mother, said: *there is good*
in you yet before placing a prayer

for the ground. Blessed America,
there is good in you yet. *In a casket*

people are sometimes born. I have told my origin
story over and over. *My parents fought, too.*

In Vietnam. They dodged Jesus, who'd
extended his hand. And so I was born

in a lunar mansion—a configuration of the moon where
my face changes in accordance with the light.

I

Big Bang Theory

In the beginning
there was me—
small creature
floating in a wet
universe. Then light
and sound and God
was there, but he looked
like my father,
like he'd been smoking
since he was a kid,
his breath the eighth
day of creation,
which was the first time
he wondered
what it meant to love
a man, what
it meant to open
his heart
to the Lord.
This is how
a universe begins:
some bloody animal
inches out of a womb
gasping for breath.
Some deity's brain
spills ink all over
a clean sheet of paper.
All of life compresses
into a single molecule—
the dotted i—everything
in the present
tense until a nonstop
explosion

scatters some matter
into planetary systems
set to embrace life.
It's a miracle
when I look back
that far and know my father
would one day sit
on our back porch
in his denim jacket
and press smoke
through the screen
door like he wanted
to make a new system
for breathing.
If it's true,
the old scriptures,
that man was made
in the image of God,
then God might be gay
and grayed with four kids
set against an infinite backdrop
of space and love and smoke.

Smoking Gun Theory

If I smoke one,
then I will smoke
two, and if I smoke
too many, I will
find myself
addicted to the way
the fire hugs
my lips, how
it doesn't
actually touch.
This is construction
in the modern age.
All the bad shit
I shove
into my body
turns into bad
memories
about my chain
smoking father,
how each time
he stepped out,
I grew
my talent
for adjusting
expectations.
The Fermi Paradox
asks us where
the hell everybody
went. Billions
of potential planets
and not a single
sign of alien contact.
In a parallel world,

my father understands
what I mean
when I say I love
my mother's cigarette
sensibility, the way
she burns through
each day a few inches
at a time, infinity
and parallels and space
just concepts
that keep men
a little busy,
the universe
one big-ass cigarette,
no lung big enough
to puff it down,
infinitely unable
to contain itself
like it's always crying
over not knowing
its parents. Maybe
they're chain smokers.
Maybe it's a really long
chain. Maybe every time
I step outside,
it becomes a little
harder to go back in.

Anagrams

I am an anagram
of my father. In America,
it is anapound. It is an archaic
system of measurement.
I have my father's eyes.
I am made of letters
I didn't learn
until I was five.
A is for assimilation,
which is an anagram
for cultural exorcism.
If I say I'm glad
I can speak English,
I mean to say
English is an anagram
for God's tongue.
I mean to say I don't believe
in people who expect
to be trusted. My father
gave me a chili pepper
and told me it was sweet.
He showed me the plant
it grew on, its stem
striking the sky
like lightning, like the pepper
that would burn my tongue
is one in a million.
Million is an anagram for poor,
which is an anagram for telling
restaurants I wasn't ten
to get the kid's buffet price
until I was fourteen. At fourteen,
lying became an anagram

for divorce. Divorce
became an anagram for beginning,
as in—In the beginning,
there was light and light
said let there be God
and God said let there be
life and my father
said let this pepper teach you
humility. There are days
where I'm bilingual
and days where I don't speak
with my parents. My father
saw my mother as an anagram
for love. This is not how it works.
Dad is an anagram for add.
I've been piling the letters
into my mouth for a long time
and I still can't make a good
anagram for love. There is evol,
which is an abbreviation
for evolve, which is an anagram
for aging, which is an anagram
running from your birth,
the start gun sounded off,
you breathing harder each step.
It is easier to be struck
by lightning than to win
the lottery. You stand
in an open field with your hands
pressed in prayer, arrowed
above your head toward the sky,
and you say light
when you mean life, and you say
God when you mean good,
and you say father
when you mean further, and you
say you when you mean I.

Or James

who ordained the holy
translation of the Bible.

Or me, little rebel—having worshipped
lesser things than God
at the grocery store
where my father asked me

to translate the English.

He seemed to shrink
in those moments, even
for exchanges so innocuous

I can only remember
the shift in focus
to me—little child—how I guided

those sounds to another sound
the way a bird grinds an insect

into mush before offering it
to its children, their tiny beaks
open—always
asking for more.

Such are the things

I worship: small creatures
that get what they want
with basic sounds.

Or James,
who told his people
God is their language

and their father
and their salvation
or else.

God Theory

The big G
stands for gravity.
It is the main thing
preventing me,
a wingless angel,
from taking flight.
No halo. No bullshit
about purity or goodness
or Godness. There isn't
a single creature
who doesn't need
to touch the ground,
and what is God
but a creature, sentient
and asking to be loved,
asking for faith in all
the things that can't be seen
about Him, which is everything,
which is a whole lot
of trust I don't have
even in myself.
Maybe this whole time
I've been looking for God
in all the wrong places.
Earth is the beast's
mouth and God is the beast.
I've spent my life
on the fringe of being
swallowed. I confess
I have never prayed.
I think God is how people
make sense of life
and death, that there must

be someone who understands
it all. That we don't just
close our eyes and disappear.
But we go to sleep
and wake up every day
to find the people around us
slowly dying. Life as a series
of extinctions. I will say this
once. I can't believe in God.
My life is not so insignificant.
If I jump right now,
the big G will bring me back
down. If I pilot a plane,
I will crash once
all the fuel burns. If I grow
wings, they will tire.
If I shout to the sky,
I will run out of breath.
I will lose my voice.
If I say God, I mean
there's a part of me
that wants someone
to tell me everything is okay.
That I'm tethered
to the ground like everyone
else. That the sky isn't filled
by some big idea, some God
who knows me better than me.

Apogee

"Let us eat what makes us holy."
—EMILY JUNGMIN YOON

I am holy tongued
for God has found his way
from my mouth,
where I have said his name
over and again.
This is how Moses
parted the Red Sea—
he said God
until the dry air
parted the water.
A strong enough thirst
becomes faith.
This is how I learned
English—chanting
the alphabet
until it felt natural,
like language
is something you
are born with
and not given.
Or taken.
Now when I try
to remember the exact
moment I stopped
thinking in Vietnamese
and how that must
have been the borderline
of my migration—on one side
me, God-blessed
and assimilated.
On the other
the boy I am trying
to remember. If it was fear

or curiosity that held me
when I first heard
English. If such forced
consumption
was bravery. I mean,
what else does a follower do
but walk
if the man they're following
splits the sea.

Quantum Jump

I am false bravado
more than I am whatever
regular bravado is,
whatever creature
could rise from its sleep
each day unchanged
by the earth's tilt,
and if I say I'm not
suicidal, then maybe
I am fooling nobody.
There's something
to be learned from
watching a fly slam
itself into a screen
catcher over and over,
the little grid
a net it just found
itself caught behind,
even if the net's been there
the whole time.
If there's a way in,
then there must be
a way out, and if
there's a way to catalog
the small bits of joy
of each day, a little
note here about catching
the fly in a cup
and letting it live
for a while longer, a note
there on how to fold
those moments
into my palms the way

children catch fireflies
and tell the little doubters
in the pews of their bodies
that the bugs will light their nights
forever, this faith, this
understanding that the tails
flickering are so much bigger
than the stars
that come out every night
when you hold them
close to your face, this
perspective a kind of science
children will believe
until they are older
and tall enough to face
the night, when the distance
separating the foot
and the sky is the smallest
it will ever be. I understand
someone invented the plane.
I understand there are many
ways to leave the ground.
I have jumped. I have hung
from a tree branch.
I have never landed
in the same spot.

Migration Theory

The horses migrate. The birds and the whales too.
They are all running from winter.

This route passed down from their mother
and their mother's mothers for so long

that it is now coded into their blood:
the grains of their muscles like maps, their bones

shaped like arrows. Always pointing. Instinct
a kind of religion where the messiah is a creature

bearing its fangs. Its face dripping. The sky opens
its mouth come winter and spits out its dead teeth.

And so we have snow. And so the runners know to run.
I have beaten my fists into the ground before. Even

on all fours, I am not much of a horse. It takes
all my strength to carry a human being. I have failed

so many of them. Them bucked off. Me bent to my knees
without a prayer to offer, waiting for them to leave. My mother

left her country. And her mother before that. Always wars.
What else was there to do but run and hope the beast starves.

Guerilla Theory

The largest primate in the world
is the white man's ego. It has learned
thousands of English words
it employs every day in an attempt
to fill the silences of the world.
Hello, child plant. Hello, human.
So began the system
of naming. So fell the Tower
of Babel. Nature took over. I saw
a monkey's face when I looked
at a cloud, but my mother couldn't
even make out the head. Someone
looked at a tree and called it a tree.
Someone else looked at a tree
and called it whatever the word
for tree is in Vietnamese,
which I don't remember anymore.
And the word for that loss
is too big to fit into a single
word. It unrooted itself from
my tongue and replanted itself
in the different dips of the English
language. I have been engaged
in guerilla warfare ever since
my first teacher had me recite
the beginnings of the alphabet.
The letters were dropped
out of bombers. I am full
of holes and dormant land mines.
So if a gorilla rises from the fox-
holes, there are no warnings.
It is the kind of predator that strikes
from behind. And when I turn

toward the drumbeat
of its feet, the loud thunder song
sung behind the trees, I see
only its path: the jungle undone,
the soil pressed a little deeper
into itself. And into me.

Notes on Translation

1. Dad pulls you aside and says *Do you want to live with your mother?* Does not offer himself up as an option. In your head this is said in English. Everything you've ever heard says the predator will leave if you can stay quiet enough. Do not make a sound. Do not let him find you.

2. The word for forget is quên.

3. If the world drowns in its own heat, then grow gills and fins. To survive is to adapt. Or maybe it is the other way around. There are so many theories as to why whales beach themselves. We think it an accident and we try to push them back into the ocean. A pail of water to keep it cool. And another. And sometimes, I think, of course it wants to live. But maybe what I mean is I want to live.

4. In fifth grade, you spell *silhouette* wrong and lose the spelling bee. When dusk hits a city, the skyline starts to merge into one as if the town is just one big building with no roads between them. What is that but a kind of love. No light to show the difference. But if you focus less on the outline and more on the darkness, you will see there are trees and animals and people. You will see where there is no shape, there can be every shape too.

5. Your mother never asks you about it.

6. Statistics say fifty percent of marriages end in divorce. I call heads every time on a flipped coin. I look right before I look left. I don't think it's fair to say I have commitment issues. I don't think it's as easy as saying *yes*. Every time I imagine myself on an altar, it feels like being spit-roasted over a fire. Only the fire is some kind of passion. But I am still some kind of pig.

7. An unrequited love is like having a needle slowly pulled from your stomach only to find a thread pushed through its loop, and the thread is stitched into your lung such that you are always trying to surface so that you can breathe like a whale.

8. My obsession with whales began in elementary school. I learned the biggest animal in the world was a blue whale and that it had no interest in swallowing me.

9. In Vietnam, there is a wet season and a dry season. The word for their difference is assimilation. The rain beats on the gravel until it becomes mud. Then it reverts when the rain leaves. I am the rock and the river—the kind of shape that changes when touched.

Light Perception

People say   *Vietnamese sounds ugly*   and I know

what they really mean   is their ears   are little UFOS

that trailblaze   over secret   military bases

abducting people   from their homes   and instilling their own

language   so I understand   it is scary

to hear something   different but let me tell you   it is scarier

to recognize a sound   but not know what it means   even a rabid
  animal

makes it clear to you   that it has been wronged   by parasites

but me   I hear my mother give up   on English every time

she talks to me   to return to her alien   tongue

and I am not prepared   to travel into space   where the stars

spread their dust   into the abyss   which is they say quiet

the science of sound   unflinching as far as we know   but how
  can it be

true I have looked upward   I have heard the ocean   stir inside me

the way it does when I hear   Vietnamese this thing I once knew
   humans are passive

forgetters and I am instinctually afraid   of growls hisses   the
   deep night

but the human tongue is something   else it is not a monster
   it can only

bite if you teach it   it can only teach you   there is more than
   one way

to see a light   if you turn your head   just slightly

the glare changes its shape   there is nothing ugly at all

The Jungle Book

I

I want the language of wolves
each howl planted in the ground

becomes a cave a lonely jungle
the holes made to hold

wolves not foxes not shrapnel
not boxes of firearms or arms

there are so many other things
to place in holes so many

ways to fill the air with sound
I grew older as I listened

to waves crash inside my mother
the amniotic fluid I swallowed

by the mouthful then floated when
I was born the wolves descended

said god bless you said it's
a boy said what's its name said it's

so beautiful I am paraphrasing
the memory imagine my own birth

the first language I heard
it's one thing to be raised by wolves

and another to be raised among them
I am just trying to grow

my fangs say my family is wolf
let us be wolf the ones

who lurk in the dark and sing
to the moon I know better

I know the silhouette
is just one shade of wolf

the shadow becomes a tree
a cliff disappears I know smaller

creatures must hold their songs
must not sing to the light

II

how r you son

how is u job

how u been

hey

are u have gf now

everything is ok for u

did u see u dad

how r u son

just take care good over there

don't work to much take care u health

are u feel better honey

no sick no more

how r u son

mom good son everything is ok for u

u don't want to answer my question

it ok love u

III

I am the fragment of the land Mom
was born on a small island and she

shipwrecked in a bottle
that holds a message says

you can make money in America
says nothing about resentment

the war over
there are only survivors

a grudge just a thing smeared to the sea-
floor there is a limit to how long

a body can float one time I watched
a documentary saw a whale's body

saw fish swim between its bones
a whole city built from the end

of its beautiful life this is how
I prefer to imagine the drowned

the boat people how the bodies wail
host that which must go on

which lives it has been thirty years
since my parents left Vietnam

they have not been back have not seen
the new cities built atop their ruin

have seen only me lay new bricks
atop my body how

I've become a foreign town
they recognize a little less each day

II

Perpetual Motion

An apple falls onto a man's head
and we have gravity.

Then we hang the head to a tree.
When that falls, we have a revolution.

Here's one where the apple turns
a white man into a snake. He tells everyone

the earth revolves around God.
God is one deep breath away

from lining our skies with his guts,
his heart beating our ears hollow.

Here's one where a black man eats
an apple and its sweetness makes him cry.

Here's one about the apple: the sky
storms when the clouds gorge themselves

on the thick sweat of our bodies. Rub two
people together and you will have rain.

Rub rain on a tree and it will grow
apples. Rub the apples against the earth

and watch worms rise from dirt. Watch
how it scatters, the bits of dark

matter inching slowly from one plot
to the next. This is how gravity works.

One person's head develops an orbit.
Then everything falls until it can't get up.

Monstro

there is nothing left

when I think of you

a tiny human steps inside me

and unravels the plastics

I have tossed to the wild

people pour small buckets of water

to keep the sand-skinned whale alive

but on land it can't even sing

all of us together can't push it back

we lift our hands to moon

to ask for a stronger tide

if I was huge I could cup it

pluck it from the earth like a tulip

every day I say I am fine

my nose grows bigger

I tug on my strings

the marionettist doesn't answer

the whale doesn't move

the sea fills its stomach

with things that cannot sing

Autopsy

I am told it is easier
to trust me
if I show you
my hands.
Imagine
for a moment
how the rib cage
looks like a second
pair of hands
nestled over
the lungs—
this a sleight
of hand. And
imagine that beneath
the bone
you can see
the heartbeat.
Imagine, even,
that it beats
for you. And then.
And then it stops.
Not the heart
but the imagining.
How easy it is to pretend
to be something
else. It is easy
to breathe life
into something inanimate.
The hard part
is keeping it alive.

Take, for instance,
my hands. I have taken
them back from you,
but now I don't know
where to put them.

String Theory

The theory of everything: There are twenty-six
versions of me blowing wind into wind. All of us
    turning our lungs inside out.

There is the bear who hibernates all summer
    until she wakes into whiteness and wonders
        where all the other bears have gone, why God

sheds His skin all winter. There is the unborn boy
    floating as a name in a woman's head. Call her Hoa.
        Call her Mom. Call her once in a while and tell her

    you could be anything, so you chose to be nothing—
godlike and infinite. Compress your being
    into a book and call it holy. Hold it to your chest

    and let your oldest testament beat its way
into your heart so your brain won't
    be the only organ that understands death.

Let that be the revision to my childhood
    where I cry a little less and eat a little more,
        where milk truly makes the bones grow

dinosaur-sized, strong and bound
    for extinction. Holy star, holy meteor,
    tell me a fable where the creatures aren't afraid

    of the author or his wicked whims. I am the same
in this realm and the next is my new mantra.
    At least one of me has found a den to crawl into

for months each year just to remind myself of the time
      I was tethered to my mother. Now, I am unsure
           if death isn't just a more permanent version of her,

      or if I'm already dead in a parallel dimension,
      my selves splintered into strings for the universe to weave
into the wind. All I want to know is when I die, if

it will be different from crawling back into the womb.

Reverse Howl

I didn't know what to make of my mother
when she cried. I kept the door closed.

I turned up my television. I built
up white noise between our silence

the way God sometimes places storm
clouds between Earth and heaven.

I have absorbed so much of my environment.
I am a good little American boy, and boys

don't cry. They don't cry wolf
when they are supposed to be the shepherd—

behind them a flock of lambs.
Even they can tell the difference

between thunder and lightning, a sob
versus silence. I have not inherited

any sort of motherness. I don't know
which one to be more afraid of: the wolf

who bares its fangs and growls, or the one
who watches me quietly from the forest—

one can swallow the sky,
and the other can spit it back out.

Child of God

I ate tteokbokki. I fell
in love. I ate mochi
and fell in love. I fell in
love eating kebab
in Berlin, and I fell in love
fishing dumplings
from a bowl of soup
in Guangzhou.

My tongue doesn't
have to explain to anyone
why it does or does
not like something.
I am a firm believer
in love at first sight.

It is like when a gazelle gives
birth in the wild—its baby
can walk the second it is born.
Love has such legs.
It can run with the herd
before it even knows
what's chasing it.

Love Theory

When I butt dial my mother, I am drunk
and trying to convince the woman

I am seeing that I am trustworthy.
She calls back three times and leaves

a voice mail before I realize my mistake.
She says she hopes everything is okay.

When I call her back, I only tell her
I'm sorry, but I can't hear you.

It was an accident. I love you
and then I hang up and wonder

if this is how we will spend the rest
of our lives, one accidental phone call

at a time. When the man selling
Korean BBQ tacos finishes setting up

and no one else is in line, I know
the night is not a mistake. The woman

I've been seeing tells me she wants
to trust me. My tongue pulls the pork

from the taco shell. When I think too much
about what I'm eating, I stop eating.

She says she wants to give us a shot,
but I think she means I need my leg

punctured so I might stay in one spot.
When I take another shot of whiskey,

it is not what anyone wanted.
If I say lover, I mean I love her.

When I say I love her, I don't know
who I'm referring to. If I say love,

I mean I want to be trusted.
I want someone to let me tie them

to a string and reduce their weight
to paper, turn them into a kite

and let me run beneath them
until they miss the easy way

the foot trusts the ground.
I want to pull them down

and be the first extension
of the earth they touch.

Anchor

I unloaded my stomach
onto the pavement again,

a gut check to push my body
to its edges—inflate it

to the point just before it pops,
or as so often happens, just after.

I have learned so much
from my mistakes. Do not pet

a dog's ass when it's not looking,
or anyone's ass for that matter.

If someone offers me a drink,
I've taken it and spilled it

into my mouth. Swallowed it
quickly. This is one way

to test how hollow you are.
Do not despair. Inside us

is enough space for even
the most grotesque-looking creatures.

The liver, the lover—

there are worse things
to spill than the stomach.

I've Lost My Umbrella Again

I forgot the rain.
Left it in the sky again.
I like when they pull tiny swords
out from under the umbrella
in movies. I hope it functions
as a normal umbrella
during the non-movie parts
of their lives. Standing
with someone beneath
an umbrella as it rains
as if you've built your own
portable world. Under there
you could do anything.
There is the obvious,
such as holding hands
or planting tiny minnows
in each puddle you walk
by so that they can grow
into big sharks. You
can imagine anything
when you share an umbrella
with someone. Even
on sunny days, it is used
to block out the light.
Look how easy it is to create
our own tiny darknesses.
I will forget my umbrella again,
and when I look for it later
I will instead find the rain.

On Kindness

My friend doesn't eat animal
meat that still looks like the animal.

The animal, dead, cannot come back
to life. At least not without

a miracle in which you can turn
your fingers into God and jigsaw

the pieces back together. With crabs
or lobsters, though, you can skip

the puzzle. I am not going to pull
a façade over anyone. I don't contain

much empathy for such things,
but I am moved by my friend who does.

She could fit a turtle into her human
shell. And not just a turtle, but a giant beach

of turtle eggs, who could then hatch
and all make it to the ocean. That world

seems a lot kinder and a lot more
beautiful. Everything eats not to live

but for joy. At some point in history,
a single organism existed—call it God

or call it a microorganism—and then
at some point it split, and some point

beyond that one of the splits looked
at the other and wanted to eat it.

These days it's called love. Or war.
These days I look at something

and it might look back.

Mantras

So what if I'm not loved.

How dumb to be the moon.

Earth isn't even the center of the solar system.

I am sick of their whispering.

I had my own crying corner as a boy.

I still have it.

The Asian man has been emasculated?

That's true if you think of masculinity as being inherently
tied to sexuality.

That's true if you think a neutered dog is no longer a dog.

I don't want to be a dog at all.

I don't want to be a "man."

My greatest fear is being cheated on.

Being a man means mangos.

Manta rays. Caiman. Snowmen.

Mandatory attendance. Amen.

I want to be loved. Amen.

I just don't know by who. Amen.

Swan Song

I've seen my father
swim once.

I watched him bow
his body into the pool

the way a swan
dips its head

beneath the surface.
He stayed under

for a long time.
When I learned

he was gay,
I thought of his head

emerging from
the other end

of the pool.
I thought of the nights

he spent with my mother,
how he held

his breath for a long
time. I thought of the time

he told me he didn't love
me. I thought of Vietnam,

how it weaves in
and out of wetness,

the rain each year
a reminder of the human

and its contract
with the land.

Holy Grail

My father changed
     his name to Henry

and became King
     of white people.

He pulled my spine
     from my back

to prove he commanded
     the holy sword.

Holy bone.
     The half-corpse

of his firstborn.
     I moved

as he willed. I danced.
     I prostrated

myself at his feet
     and said Lord.

And Father. Holy
     Father. I rose

when he introduced
     me to his partner,

an old white man
     who reads books

about Buddhism.
　　　This was the first step

toward enlightenment:
　　　find a Vietnamese man

who has left one
　　　body for another.

The new body a grail
for a gay immigrant

father. I am just a reminder
of the old ways. The boat

people didn't answer
　　　the ocean's song

when they rowed. The ones
　　　who did went under.

All of them leaving
　　　behind a world

I will never understand.
　　　This is what I mean

when I say I am spineless.
　　　When I said my father

took it from me, I meant
　　　to say God exists,

and he is my father,
　　　life bringer, holy

immigrant. My body now
　　　my own forever.

III

The Moth

Even humans know to follow
light. We say *At the end of the tunnel*
there must be light when all evidence
suggests otherwise. I'll close my eyes
one day and never see a light again.
I'll jump from the ground
and become a tiny bug outside
someone's window, catching
their attention for a second
before they blink and I am off
to the shadow of some corner
they won't think to look to.

Dog Meat

Vietnamese people eat dog,   but not me.
       I am not a dog eater.
              The other kids lied all the time. Said I ate
       dogs, so my father taught me what to do
       with the lie.
First, walk the dog   up and down
our trailer park—this, too,   a dog park.
       When the dog barks,
that means it wants to sit down.
          Prepare the cutting board. Place the   lie
on the old plastic board   stained the color
of the dog's   teeth.   Take out the cleaver,
         and take care to not cut yourself—
              it is important to not bleed.
              Do not let your blood drip
                   into the lie.
      Rinse the body under the sink.
The meat isn't dog.   It never is
       anymore.
Some things are   lost
when you cross   the Pacific Ocean.
       The dog drowns. The meat rots.
Dissect the lie. Bring the cleaver down.
It should plop the way a dog plops
       when it is too tired to walk.
I have seen this before. Belly to earth.
          Earth to belly.
The same position I take
       when my father leaves for the first time.
The night quiet.   The dog quiet.
I waited with my tail up,   like a roast—spit fired.
The quiet spun me until he came home
         late in the night—the door

          whimpering.   I wanted to bark
at him.   Bare my fangs.   But my tongue
          hung there,   salivating
until it was too late.   My father found   me.
He took the cleaver—the one for the lie—
                    and offered it to me. I took it.
                    He showed me his own. Together
          we hung ourselves   on meat hooks
              and cut the fat from our bodies.

Almost

Bags of ice drip from the back of a small bike
in Vietnam. The exhaust pipe rumbles. The man
sweats. My tongue melts. We are lucky we are not tiny
starving polar bears slipping off the last refuge
of ice into the black asphalt. The open
ocean. Or I should say we are lucky
the coming flood is incremental.
We are lucky to share this moment—
him delivering the bags of ice
before they melt, and me having returned
to my parents' birthplace, which is to me
an almost-home in that I am almost
melting. An old woman sells a child
a snack. Her mother hands her some cash.
The old woman doesn't melt. The bike
doesn't melt. We are lucky to be held
together by bodies which are so difficult
to melt. We are similar in our almost-melting,
just as the sounds of the café I am sitting in
almost melt into me the way a song's name sits
on the tip of your tongue when you can't
remember it. I will never fully know
the sounds because I am lucky to have left
the melting: my mother lucky
to have a family that didn't need to sell
dried pieces of squid, which is a thing
I almost-understand—the old woman
squatting in the street. In Vietnam
I am the piece of ice that stays
on the bike. I am the child
chewing on the dried squid. I am lucky
it is dead and cannot escape into the wet

air, where the Vietnamese people swim
and their voices distort just slightly—I can
almost understand them. I can almost
piece my tongue back together.
I can almost stop the melting.

Crucifixion

If I drop napalm
on an ant hill, of course
they'll scatter. Some will die.
Of course people look
like ants from above.
Of course my parents
want to return to be buried
in their home country.
But I am not my parents.
I do not want to return
to my birth in a hospital
with the word *Saint* in its name,
the other details remnants
of colonization: white hands
wiping blood from my skin,
snipping the foreskin from my dick.
Maybe one of the doctors
said a quick prayer
in my name, called me Baby
because he couldn't pronounce
the name my parents scrawled
onto the piece of paper.
Maybe I'm obligated
to think of Jesus
from time to time.
This is a lot to ask of me.
I think about Vietnam
from time to time.
I hope that's the same
thing—that on the third day,
it, too, will rise, the foxholes
on its hands no longer bloody.

Apocalypse with Crumbs

God needed to chew
with his mouth closed,
such that little crumbs
didn't fly off
his tongue and turn
into little birds
not out of desire
but necessity,
such that dinosaurs
aren't just the lick
of drool running
from His
mouth, which swallowed
the Cretaceous era in one gulp.
Evolution is Michelangelo's
The Creation of Adam
except with a T-Rex's claw
touching a bird's wing
and the bird's wing
touching the sun
which touched Icarus
all the same.
Folly a repeating
strand of DNA—see all
the wars in human history.
See all those people
building upon each other's
deaths. See me in my underwear
grinding my teeth
against a Nature Valley granola bar—
all the crumbs
an avalanche. What a fine display
of hunger. Of avarice.

I am watching the world's
next great extinction. The oceans
are rising. The air is warming.
So much of the earth is now
being consumed by humans.
I can only hope that once
we are swallowed, again
something with wings
and a pleasant morning song
will drip back toward the earth.

What Kind of Morning

comes so early? All this light
as if a little Moses basket
would be waiting at my door
with some child who would grow up
to tell me the things
I cannot do. What a horrible
gift. There was a time
I loved the sun. There are so many
things I used to love. At five,
I broke into a chest of toys
with a pair of chopsticks.
My mother snapped
the chopsticks in half
over my hands. She didn't
like to be woken up
either. How easy it is
to make two things out
of one thing. If you break
your morning in half,
you get two chances
to pick up little Moses.
Maybe you get two Moseses.
Maybe we'd get double
the commandments.
Honor thy father
and thy mother, and yourself
and yourself. Double
a good thing and it's hard
for that to go wrong. Twice
the love. Twice the belief
that nothing could backfire.
It's easier to fly with two wings
than one. A bird with one wing

is a broken proverb. Two
in the bush is two in the bush.
Let them do as creatures do—
this, perhaps, one of the new
commandments. Just this morning
I woke up and there was nothing
at the door, but it was nice
to look. I have faith in a day
where something comes so early
it will feel like it's late,
like I should have known about it
a long time ago.

The Namings

I used to think I could do anything
with enough effort—throw a rope
at the night and lasso in the moon,
or jump from a tree
and beat my arms into wings
like an owl, its feathers nothing
more than decoration, nothing my naked
arms couldn't match. I was an imaginative
child. An imbecile in some circles.
It is not nice to call someone names.
I was the name-caller. I said Little White
Sickle to the moon. I said Big Head Bird
to the owl. I said Mom, and I said Dad.
I thought if I shouted these names loud
enough, then someone would respond.
These days I have seen my best
efforts fail. All the love I've poured
into a person. Or them into me.
How I've failed to open myself
properly to receive their names.
Love. Love bird. I have been called
so many names. I have so many
identities I never meant to adopt.
In the dark, the owls hoot at each other
and I shout back: me, me, me.

Silhouettes

A crow perches inside me.

Actually, it is a whale. It is hard to tell
by touch alone. Nothing I own ever looks
me properly in the eye. Sometimes

a loud caw at dusk feels
like the largest mammal on Earth.

A deep breath out the blowhole

into my stomach. One second it swims
and the next it is a small extension
of a tree. This is a kind of beginning—

a finger puppet show. The light
dancing around my hands.

Me dancing alone on a stem.

A persimmon blooms.
A boy learns a song and plants
it in an orchard. Inside of me

the large creatures change their shapes
to fit. A blackbird. An organ.

Animals with no names. I send them off
into the world daily. Little *sadness*
takes flight. *Love* is a brave child.

These things take the shape
of their containers.

I don't have to do anything
to hold them.

Ode to Working

at Taco Bell
with your mother
who is called Mom
by all your coworkers
so you wonder
if you should call her
something else
to make them think
you have that special
mother-son bond
you see on the *Discovery*
Channel when blue
whales offer a hundred
gallons of milk
each day to their offspring
and show them
the migratory routes
coded into their DNA,
which is not too different
from your mother
sliding you a little extra food
when you take your break.
Family legends say
you were born there,
straight out of a bag of ground
beef in spite of regulations,
and the meat, if you
can call it that, tasted
fine, and in spite
of the strict codes
your boss maintains,
the plastic
bag of meat still looks

like a plastic bag of meat,
which is to say it
looks like it just crawled
out of some creature's
womb, which is why you lie
in bed sometimes
in the middle of night
when your stomach growls
for a third meal and think
about all the nasty shit
that must be part of your
genetic composition—the cattle
flesh minced and salvaged, picked
clean off the bone, the mystery
chemicals a mixture of sweat
and blood, all the stupid
things you've placed
into your mouth, all the times
you said Mom and she turned
her head to look at you,
to see what you wanted.

Theory

A cow jumped over the moon
and became a children's
tale. It's why cheese is filled
with moon craters.
It's why drinking milk fills
out the wax and wane nature
of the stomach,
which is to say children are right
to fear the dark.
Here's to father sky,
to mother earth.
Here's to my boy/girl
understanding of the human
condition. I've made
a lot of poor decisions.
I don't drink milk.
My bones collected
my father's smoke instead.
When I snapped my elbow,
the smog seeped out.
My mother drove me
to the hospital and told me
she was right,
that I should have drank
my milk. This is how a fable
begins. You experience
something for the first time
like a newborn baby
trying to make the right sounds
to get someone to understand
you need something.
You don't imagine yourself

crying. But there's the first breath.
There's light. You sing a song
to the doctors and nurses:
you cry where, where,
until you fall asleep.

Penultimates

The day before you died.

A wildebeest chewing on grass. The sun the only thing in the sky.

The sky is gray and wet.

The moment before is now the second to last moment.

The phone is ringing.

There is always a closer moment.

A rustle in the tall grass behind it. A bubble from the watering hole.

I say *I love you.* You say *I know.*

Every moment leads to another.

I tell myself this ache will pass. Then it is my knee. Then my back.

It doesn't die immediately.

Even after it passes, I am waiting for myself to catch up to my body.

This is what a ghost is.

Even after I've caught up to my body, there is no way to keep it from moving ahead.

I am always almost there.

I am always there.

Acknowledgments

This book wouldn't be possible without the support I've received. I am grateful to be here with you.

Thank you to my parents, my brothers, and my sister for being there each in their own unique manner.

Thank you to Jon Davies and the rest of the team at the University of Georgia Press for giving a physical body for these poems.

Thank you to Kyle Dargan and the National Poetry Series for selecting my book for this tremendous opportunity.

Thank you to my many mentors—Diane Wakoski, Ross Gay, Stacey Lynn Brown, Adrian Matejka—and the rest of the faculty at Indiana University's MFA program for both your guidance and patience.

Thank you to the many friends and colleagues who shared a very particular time and space with me in Indiana, especially my fellow cohort Britt Ashley, Shayla Lawson, Trevor Mackesey, and Scott Miles. Thank you also to everyone not in my graduating class, including Paul Asta, Doug Paul Case, Su Cho, Jessica Franck, Clint Frazier, Steph Horvath, J. T. Howard, Joshua Johnston, Keith Leonard, Lisa Low, Catie Lycurgus, Michael Mlekoday, Emily Myrick, Randi Ocena, Sam Ocena, Danni Quintos, and Maggie Su.

Thank you to the many writers whose feedback and friendship helped shape this book. I know feedback is a labor beyond just love, so I am always deeply grateful to those of you who've spent time talking to me about my poems, especially Eloisa Amezcua, Jericho Brown, Wo Chan, Meg Freitag, Edgar Kunz, Sally Wen Mao, Safiya Sinclair, and Jenny Xie.

Thank you to my Kundiman family for giving a space to be me. You have my support always.

Thank you to the boys from the basement, NPNG, and the clowns. To Jennifer Nina and to Marianne Chan. To my many esports friends but especially Tina Jo and Joe Thorn—without all of you, my life and this book would be much less interesting.

Thank you to Katie Moulton for cheering for St. Louis sports teams. Someone has to do it.

Thank you to Cathy Yang, known anime lover, for watching anime, which you love, with me.

Thank you to my twin, Leslie Marie Aguilar, for crying about our friendship.

Thank you to Tia Clark. I lost the friendship check you sent me. Sorry.

And lastly, thank you to Emily Jungmin Yoon for being my first reader and editor. Thank you for the good tips and for being my best friend.

The author thanks the following publications in which these poems first appeared:

Lunar Mansions: *American Poetry Review*
Big Bang Theory: *Academy of American Poets*
Smoking Gun Theory: *[PANK]*
Anagrams: *Ploughshares*
Or James: *Tayo Literary Magazine*
God Theory: *[PANK]*
Apogee: *American Poetry Review*
Quantum Jump: *Sugar House Review*
Guerilla Theory: *Kenyon Review*
Notes on Translation: *Cincinnati Review*
Light Perception: *Hyperallergic*
The Jungle Book: *The Rumpus*
Perpetual Motion: *Pleiades*
Monstro: *The Offing*
Autopsy: *The Offing*
String Theory: *Tayo Literary Magazine*
Reverse Howl: *The Rumpus*

Love Theory: *Day One*
On Kindess: *American Poetry Review*
Mantras: *The New Republic*
Swan Song: *The Margins*
Holy Grail: *The Nation*
Dog Meat: *The Racist Sandwich Podcast*
Almost: *The Offing*
Crucifixion: *[PANK]*
Apocalypse with Crumbs: *Georgia Review*
The Namings: *American Poetry Review*
Silhouettes: *Poetry Magazine*
Ode to Working: *Southern Indiana Review*
Theory: *Muzzle Magazine*
Penultimates: *TriQuarterly*